BOOK ANALYSIS

Never Let Me Go

BY KAZUO ISHIGURO

BOOK ANALYSIS

By Dylan Alling

Never Let Me Go
BY KAZUO ISHIGURO

Bright
≡**Summaries**.com

KAZUO ISHIGURO	9
NEVER LET ME GO	13
SUMMARY	17

Part One – Hailsham
Part Two – the Cottages
Part Three – Donations

CHARACTER STUDY	25

Kathy
Ruth
Tommy
Miss Emily
Madame
Miss Lucy

ANALYSIS	33

Humanity
Materialism
Memories and style

FURTHER REFLECTION	41
FURTHER READING	47

KAZUO ISHIGURO

CONTEMPORARY BRITISH NOVELIST

- **Born in Nagasaki, Japan in 1954.**
- **Notable works:**
  - *A Pale View of Hills* (1982), novel
  - *The Remains of the Day* (1989), novel
  - *The Buried Giant* (2015), fantasy novel

Kazuo Ishiguro is a British novelist who was born in Nagasaki, Japan on 8 November 1954. He moved to Britain with his family at a young age and was educated in Surrey and subsequently at the universities of Kent and East Anglia. Most of Ishiguro's novels place the reader in the passenger's seat of one protagonist's extensive journey. Most of his work employs first-person narration, which is used to delve into the personal memories of one figure. Ishiguro creates a mental portrait of his protagonist in addition to a social portrait of the contemporary society that surrounds and drives that story. That particular social setting may be based on fantasy (as in *The Buried Giant*), it may be futuristic (*Never Let Me Go*), or it might be a pre-war or post-war historical setting, as in *The Remains of the Day*. Ishiguro embraces his Japanese heritage and the alternate perspective that his Japanese upbringing has provided him with, as can be seen in his choice to set his 1986 novel *An Artist of the Floating World* in post-World War II Japan. Ishiguro's work deals with remembrance and nostalgia, acceptance of the past and human failure, and the examination of the basic value systems found in certain societies. Ishiguro is a critically acclaimed: he won the Man Booker Prize in 1989 and received the Nobel Prize in Literature in 2017.

NEVER LET ME GO

LOVE AND LOSS IN A DYSTOPIAN ENGLAND

- **Genre:** dystopian science fiction novel
- **Reference edition:** Ishiguro, K. (2006) *Never Let Me Go*. Croydon: Faber and Faber.
- **1st edition:** 2005
- **Themes:** humanity, love, coming of age, mortality, ethics, friendship

Never Let Me Go is Kazuo Ishiguro's sixth novel. It was published in 2005, and in addition to being named by *Time* magazine as the best novel of the year, it was shortlisted for the Man Booker Prize, the Arthur C. Clarke Award and the National Book Critics Circle Award.

The story takes place during the 1990s in the England of a parallel world, one in which creating and raising cloned humans to serve as organ donors is a widely used and accepted medical procedure. The story follows the life of an organ donor named Kathy, who we witness graduate through the various institutions of the donations programme. We follow her as she grows up and experiences various facets of life, such as changing friendships, sex, discovering music and art, and love. Her final confrontation with the harsh truth about the science-driven society in which she lives leaves us with ethical questions concerning the nature of being human.

SUMMARY

PART ONE – HAILSHAM

Our novel is set in a parallel version of the England of the late 1990s. Our narrator and protagonist, Kathy H, is a 31-year-old woman who lives in a world in which some human beings are cloned for the purpose of donating their organs. Kathy is one such donor. However, at the opening point of the story she is not yet a donor but a "carer", meaning that she is a sort of donor guardian, driving the donors to various medical facilities and taking care of them following their operations. After a number of operations the donors die, or "complete", as it is termed.

Kathy delves into her past, and she begins by narrating detailed memories of her upbringing at an institution called Hailsham, which is located in an unnamed part of the English countryside. At first Hailsham appears to be a normal institution: Kathy and her friends gossip, play sports, have classes and make art. However, as Kathy's description progresses we find that Hailsham is home to some curious rules and customs. One such custom is the so-called "Exchanges" that take place there. The "Exchanges" are a sort trade exhibition in which the students present pieces of art that they have created and are subsequently able to 'purchase' pieces of art that their fellow classmates have produced. Due to these "Exchanges", the emphasis on producing art weighs heavily on the students of Hailsham. For this reason, when one of Kathy's teachers – or "guardians" – named Miss Lucy tells her close friend Tommy that it does not matter whether or not he is creative enough to produce art for these exhibitions, both Tommy and Kathy are left in a state of bafflement.

This is the first in the series of strange occurrences that mark Kathy's memory of her time spent at Hailsham. The next curious incident revolves around a mysterious character known at this point only as "Madame". Madame is one of the directors of the institution but will only visit a couple of times a year for the sole purpose of selecting the finest pieces of art exhibited in the Exchanges and putting them into her "Gallery". Alongside the rarity of her visits, Madame is a mysterious figure because, unlike the other guardians who interact and engage with the students, she is outwardly fearful of them.

In contrast to the Exchanges, where the students can only walk away with things created by their peers, Hailsham also hosts "Sales", where the students are given the chance to purchase objects that come from the outside world, such as clothes, toys and music. At one of these events, Kathy buys a cassette tape of Judy Bridgewater, with a song titled *Never Let Me Go*. She is fond of the song and listens to it while slowly swaying to the rhythm as she holds an imaginary baby tightly to her chest. Kathy creates this fantasy on the basis that neither her nor any of the donors in the donations programme are permitted to have children. As Kathy plays out her make-believe fantasy she is spotted by Madame, who freezes in the doorway to watch her, and then begins to sob.

Although the notion of having children is entirely unthinkable to the Hailsham students, they do fantasise about possible "dream futures", such as becoming Hollywood actors. On one of these occasions, Kathy recounts how Miss Lucy disabuses the students of that dream. She makes clear that the Hailsham students are brought into this world for the sole purpose of donating their vital organs. Their future has been decided. Part One finishes with the notice that Miss Lucy has been dismissed from Hailsham and will not return.

PART TWO – THE COTTAGES

When Kathy reaches the age of 15, she leaves Hailsham for another institution: an old converted farmhouse named the Cottages. Kathy's closest friends Ruth and Tommy accompany her to the Cottages, and it is here that the relationship between the three of them suffers regular highs and lows. Ruth tries to impress the older "veteran" students at the Cottages by imitating their behaviour, while Kathy explores her sexual curiosity, seeking out available pornographic magazines in her free time.

At this point, two of the veterans claim that on a trip in Norfolk they saw a "possible" for Ruth, meaning the person from whom a particular student was cloned. Tommy, Ruth, Kathy and two veterans decide to investigate this "possible" and undertake their own excursion to Norfolk. They enjoy their trip as they delight in strolling through the toys and cosmetics of a Woolworths store and contemplating the peaceful paintings in a nearby art gallery. However, this joy is overshadowed by their disappointment at confirming that Ruth's "possible" is most certainly not her clone model. Ruth's disappointment turns to anger and she lashes out at the others in frustration, asking why they would even pursue this "possible" when they know that they are cloned from the "trash" of society: prostitutes, beggars and convicts.

Back at the Cottages, Tommy broods over a rumour which claims that if two donors prove they are truly in love, then they are able to defer their donations for up to three years and can thus live happily in each other's company for that time. He theorises that this is why Madame's Gallery exists: to be able to confirm through two students' artwork that their souls are aligned for love. To be able to qualify for this "deferral", Tommy begins producing drawings, which Ruth humiliates him for. The friendship between Ruth, Tommy and Kathy unravels as they graduate from the Cottages to become carers and donors.

PART THREE - DONATIONS

Many years later, Kathy is a qualified and successful carer. During one of her drives between two medical centres, she runs into a former Hailsham student who gives Kathy the idea of becoming Ruth's carer, as Ruth is now a weakened and fragile donor stationed in a nearby recovery centre. Kathy becomes Ruth's carer, and they take an excursion to an old fishing boat that has been stranded on the marshes. It happens to be near the recovery centre at which Tommy is currently stationed, and so the three of them visit the old boat together. Ruth apologises for keeping Tommy and Kathy apart, and says that if there is any truth to the deferral theory, then Tommy and Kathy would have a real chance at achieving it.

Ruth 'completes' on her subsequent donation, and Kathy becomes Tommy's carer. They visit Madame and find that Miss Emily lives at the same residence. The two head guardians lamentably explain that the deferral rumour is utterly false, and that the "Gallery" was in fact part of a wider campaign to prove the barbarity of the donations programme by showing that clone donors were indeed fully human with souls and emotions. We learn that Madame and Miss Emily had been fighting in debates around the country against the donations programme. However, a shift in public opinion resulted in the closing of Hailsham and meant that their efforts were in vain.

During Kathy and Tommy's drive back, Tommy has one of his old tantrums. Back at the recovery centre, Tommy decides to change carer before embarking on his next donation, after which he 'completes'. The final image of the novel shows Kathy standing by a tree, imagining that its branches are collecting all of the things she has lost in her life.

CHARACTER STUDY

KATHY

Kathy is the narrator and protagonist of *Never Let Me Go*. Curiously, there is little to no mention of the physical characteristics of her and her clone peers. Instead, our understanding of her is based on her habitual actions and emotional reactions to the events that transpire in the novel. Kathy is curious, contemplative and loyal: she remains a steadfast companion to Ruth throughout her life, and although she is frequently irritated by Ruth's behaviour, she chooses to forgive her and points out her errors, thus encouraging Ruth to be genuine and true to herself and her past. At the Cottages, Kathy is unbothered by the desire to impress the older "veterans" to gain a higher social standing. She finds joy in contemplating art, solitary walks and having fun with her friends. Kathy is a dreamer, revelling in her little moments of fantasy, but she is also in some sense a conformist: she follows the rules and the path set out for her and does not stir herself or others to any sort of rebellion or revolt.

RUTH

Ruth is Kathy's closest female friend. Among their friendship circle, Ruth is the undisputed leader, as she is controlling and calls the shots for the others to follow. As illustrated when she humiliates Tommy by making fun of his somewhat infantile drawings, she can be mean and piercing with her comments and can on occasion subject those around her to sudden flashes of anger, irritation and jealousy. However, the reader gradually realises that this tough exterior covers a fragile interior. Ruth is insecure, and her willingness to pretend to know things that in fact she does not (for example when she boasts to Kathy of her chess expertise, only for Kathy to realise that Ruth has not the faintest idea of the rules) highlights her inclination to buy into fantasies. It is Ruth who cherishes most strongly the ideas of having a "dream future" and locating her "possible", and after failing to find it in Norfolk, she is visibly morally deflated. Ultimately, Ruth is a good-natured individual, and before dying she apologetically bestows her best wishes on Kathy and Tommy.

TOMMY

Tommy is Kathy's other lifelong companion, and lover. As shown by his insistence on finding and purchasing Kathy's lost Judy Bridgewater cassette tape, he is considerate and tender. Like her, he is a follower of the rules but is also inquisitive and prone to dreaming. Tommy cultivates the "deferral" theory, which shows his belief in true love and his aspiration for a better future. One of Tommy's defining features is his tendency to have temperamental fits. In both his younger years at Hailsham and as an adult, he experiences tantrums which are triggered by intense feelings of emotion, whether that emotion be humiliation (as when he is excluded from the football team selection) or disappointment (after discovering that there is no possibility of a deferral).

MISS EMILY

Miss Emily is the head guardian of Hailsham. In contrast to the students, Miss Emily and the other guardians are indeed given physical descriptions. Miss Emily is an older woman with silver hair, a straight back and a soft-spoken but direct manner of speech. She inspires fear in the students but also elicits respect and fosters an overall feeling of safety at the institution. Her actions are just and her mind is sharp: Ruth claims that "Miss Emily had an intellect you could slice logs with" (p. 43). The most revealing episode of the novel concerning Miss Emily is when Kathy and Tommy visit her to discuss the "deferral" theory and she discloses the true purpose of her work at Hailsham: to create as positive a life as possible for donors and to campaign against the cruelty of the donations programme. Here her character is cleared of any suspicion that might suggest she is malicious. She is honest, and her fight to prove the humanity of Kathy and those like her demonstrates her empathetic and compassionate nature.

MADAME

Throughout the majority of the novel, the character of Madame is shrouded in mystery. It is unknown whether she is French or Belgian, she is tall and slim, she has short hair, and she is always seen wearing a sharp grey suit. One of her distinguishing characteristics is that she would never engage with Hailsham students. Kathy and the other students concluded that Madame was simply afraid of them, and they confirmed this by surprising her in the hallway and finding an expression of fear and disgust cross her face. As with Miss Emily, we learn the most about Madame when Kathy and Tommy go to visit her. She is an activist and reveals that the purpose of her "Gallery" was to showcase pieces of art made by the donors to prove their inner humanity. She is emotionally troubled, and the fear that the students saw in her face was rooted in her empathetic despair at their situation. Her broken-heartedness surfaces when she weeps at the sight of Kathy dancing while clutching an invisible baby to her breast, and again at the end when she can offer no solution to Kathy and Tommy's plea.

MISS LUCY

Miss Lucy is a guardian at Hailsham. She has a short, robust and athletic figure and black hair. Miss Lucy is important in development of the novel's plot because it is her conversation with

Tommy – in which she tells him that it is okay not to be creative as she shakes with rage – that sparks Tommy and Kathy's curiosity to learn more about Hailsham and what takes place there. Miss Lucy attempts to be honest with the donors, from revealing to them that she had once smoked (forbidden at Hailsham) to speaking frankly with them about the fact that their futures are fixed. This approach is not in line with the way Miss Emily and Madame want to run the institution, and so Miss Lucy is dismissed from Hailsham.

ANALYSIS

HUMANITY

At the heart of this novel is the question of what it means to be human. Ishiguro wrote it in the early 2000s, soon after scientists had successfully cloned the first mammal – Dolly the sheep – in 1996. *Never Let Me Go* raises questions as to the social repercussions of cloning. No one doubts that the prospect of being able to provide perfect organ donations for sufferers of accidents and diseases is an attractive one, but equally no one can refute that creating cloned humans for this purpose alone is inhumane. A human being, whether a 'normal' one or a clone, is still a human being with emotional and sensitive capacities. Ishiguro shows his by using specific character motifs and behaviours to clearly identify the humanity of the novel's principal characters:

- **Sex:** As the novel charts the coming of age of a group of adolescents, it is no surprise that sex is a prominent theme. Kathy frequently relates to us the attitude towards sex taken by her and her colleagues, and often reflects on her intense sexual urges and desires. But her interest in sex exceeds normal adolescent curiosity: she experiences sexual feelings so intensely that she believes that she has been cloned from a pornographic model, and thus searches for her "possible" in the porn magazines left around at the Cottages. Sex is a fundamental human instinct, and Ishiguro has quite possibly linked the theme of sex to the character of Kathy to underscore the humanity within her.

- **Emotion:** Aside from sexual instinct, another marker of humanity is the capacity to experience emotion. Kathy and the other donors in the novel find themselves in an environment in which they must supress their emotions because they are not helpful toward their societal purpose. Donors are created solely to donate their organs, so there is no utility in their being sad at the loss of their colleagues. As such, at the end of the novel when Kathy loses both her lover Tommy and her best friend Ruth, she has no emotional outlet provided to her, and so simply returns to her car to drive off "to wherever it was I was supposed to be" (p. 282). In the face of this disturbing emotional stoicism, Ishiguro offers to the reader one recurring motif which compensates for Kathy's resignation: Tommy's tantrums. Both the opening and closing of the novel are accompanied by episodes of Tommy having temperamental outbursts. This structural unity and the rich detail with which Tommy's tantrums are described serve to emphasise this motif, and perhaps suggest a piercing humanness to these uncontrolled outbursts of emotion.

- **Search for origins:** Another distinctly human preoccupation shared by Kathy and the other clones is the search for one's origins. In the construction of their sense of identity, humans feel compelled to know where they came from. In Ishiguro's novel, the typical search to discover who one's ancestors are is replaced by the donors' mission to find their clone model. A failure to identify one's place of origin causes a feeling of unsettlement, and indeed the "possible" theory that circulates among the Hailsham students causes anguish, as shown by Kathy's compulsive search for her clone model in pornographic magazines and

Ruth's dejection at failing to find her model in Norfolk.

MATERIALISM

Material objects hold a very important place in the novel. From as early as Kathy's Hailsham memories of the Sales, there is an evident fascination with physical things. The music on Kathy's Judy Bridgewater cassette tape opens a window for her to dream, and later in the novel her rediscovery of the tape cements her relationship with Tommy and is quite simply a moment of joy for her. When Kathy initially loses the tape and Ruth tries to cheer her up by buying her an alternate cassette tape, *Twenty Classic Dance Tunes*, Kathy treasures it as a heartfelt reminder of her. She does not listen to it, as it is a purely symbolic and sentimental possession. To further emphasise the importance of objects we need not look beyond the "Gallery". This collection of student artwork symbolises much more than a warm friendship: it is an assortment of items that are used to prove that students have *souls*; in other words, it is a symbol of humanity. One may ask why Ishiguro has chosen to imbue physical belongings with so much meaning, and to answer this we might recur to the notion of loss. The life that has been mapped out for Kathy and the other donors is one of loss: they are disconnected from their origins, they are separated from one another in such a strict way that not even love can interrupt this separation, and they even lose the one place they might have called home, Hailsham. Confronted with this sense of loss, physical objects become a method of *holding on*. Kathy's desire to hold on to her past is well illustrated by the final scene of the novel, in which she contemplates a tree in an open field, imagining that the tree's branches are catching all of the things that she has ever lost.

MEMORIES AND STYLE

Never Let Me Go is a journey through one person's memories. There are certain fragments in the novel, such as the opening of Chapter Four when Kathy states "I've been getting this urge to order all these old memories" (p. 37), that remind us of this fact. The narrative has been mentally constructed by one person and is therefore subject to imperfections and some disorder. The novel often jumps back and forth in time in the space of a couple of lines. The register is informal and the style colloquial, as shown by Kathy's constant use of contractions ("For the most part being a carer's suited me fine" p. 203). These elements combine to create a sense of individuality and personality. A novel that addresses humanity and humanness would be much less effective if it were written with distance from the personal thoughts and preoccupations of a human mind with which we can empathise.

FURTHER REFLECTION

SOME QUESTIONS TO THINK ABOUT...

- What effect does setting the novel in the England of the late 1900s have? Given that *Never Let Me Go* delves into science fiction, why might the novel be more or less effective if it were set in a completely fictitious place and time?
- A title is an important textual element to a work. Reflect on why Ishiguro might have chosen the title *Never Let Me Go*, which is the name of the Judy Bridgewater song that Kathy enjoys.
- Discuss the fact that Kathy and the other clones are not given physical descriptions, while the remaining characters, such as the guardians, are. What might this suggest about divisions among the different groups of characters in the novel?
- Near the end of the story, Kathy Tommy and Ruth take a field trip to visit an old boat that

has been left unattended in the middle of the marshes. What could this image be a symbol for?
- During Part Two of the novel, which is set primarily at the Cottages, Kathy notes that many of the veterans imitate certain behaviours taken from Hollywood television actors. Comment on the references to and role of pop culture in *Never Let Me Go*.
- When Kathy tells Miss Emily that Madame was always afraid of her and the other students back at Hailsham, Miss Emily replies "We're *all* afraid of you. I myself had to fight back my dread of you almost every day. I was at Hailsham" (p. 264). This is quite an emotionally charged and thought-provoking comment. What do you think Miss Emily means by it?
- Considering the structure of the novel, does it seem to progress is a natural fashion? Did you feel that the novel was leading up to its ending in a predictable way?
- Think about the practical dilemma that Ishiguro has created: if a member of your family were in a life-threating situation and in need of an organ donation, would you agree for the donated organ to come from a clone,

specifically created for this purpose and whom you would never confront at any point before or after the donation?

We want to hear from you!
Leave a comment on your online library
and share your favourite books on social media!

FURTHER READING

REFERENCE EDITION

- Ishiguro, K. (2006) *Never Let Me Go*. Croydon: Faber and Faber.

ADDITIONAL SOURCES

- Wong, C. F. (2005) *Kazuo Ishiguro (Series: Writers and their Work)*. Liverpool: Liverpool University Press.

ADAPTATIONS

- *Never Let Me Go*. (2010) [Film]. Mark Romanek. Dir. UK: DNA Films, Channel Four Films, Fox Searchlight Pictures.

Bright ≡Summaries.com

BOOK ANALYSIS

More guides to rediscover your love of literature

- **Animal Farm** by George Orwell
- **The Stranger** by Albert Camus
- **Harry Potter and the Sorcerer's Stone** by J.K. Rowling
- **The Silence of the Sea** by Vercors
- **Antigone** by Jean Anouilh
- **The Flowers of Evil** by Baudelaire

www.brightsummaries.com

Although the editor makes every effort to verify the accuracy of the information published, BrightSummaries.com accepts no responsibility for the content of this book.

© BrightSummaries.com, 2018. All rights reserved.

www.brightsummaries.com

Ebook EAN: 9782808012638

Paperback EAN: 9782808012645

Legal Deposit: D/2018/12603/387

Cover: © Primento

Digital conception by Primento, the digital partner of publishers.

Printed in Great Britain
by Amazon